STRENGTH**AND**MOBILITY
EXERCISES FOR
RUNNERS

Over 50 Effective Exercises to Improve Running Performance and Prevent Injury

JASON**CURTIS**

FUNDAMENTAL**LIFESTYLE**

Strength and Mobility Exercises for Runners

Over 50 Effective Exercises to Improve Running Performance and Prevent Injury

Published by **www.fundamental-lifestyle.com**

ISBN: 978-1-911267-79-9

Copyright © 2018 Jason Curtis

The moral right of this author has been asserted.

www.fundamental-lifestyle.com

Find us on Facebook: **/5sfitnessuk**

Instagram: **5s_fitness**

www.fundamental-lifestyle.com

Cover Image Copyright – Shutterstock: lzf

Contents

Disclaimer

The exercises provided by Jason Curtis / Fundamental Lifestyle and associated websites are for educational purposes only, and should not be interpreted as a specific treatment plan or course of action. Exercise is not without its risks and this, or any other exercise program, may result in injury. Risks include (but are not limited to) injury, aggravation of a pre-existing condition, or the adverse effects of over-exertion, such as muscle strain, abnormal blood pressure, fainting, disorders of heartbeat and, in very rare instances, heart attack.

To reduce the risk of injury, please consult a healthcare provider for appropriate advice and safety instructions. The exercise instruction and advice presented are in no way intended as a substitute for medical / personal training consultation. Jason Curtis / Fundamental Changes disclaims any liability from and in connection with this program. As with any exercise program, if at any point during your workout you begin to feel faint, dizzy, or have physical discomfort, you should stop immediately and consult a physician.

Jason Curtis / Fundamental Changes does not provide specific or personalised medical, fitness, strength, or training advice, and is not engaged in providing medical services. This book and associated video instruction does not replace consultation with qualified a health or medical professional who sees you in person.

Introduction

Whenever I ask a client about their fitness level, their usual response is either, "Terrible, I can't run" or "Good, I can run well."

This attitude is often caused by people perceiving fitness as the ability to run, and because running is often a go-to method used for developing health and fitness.

Not only is running great for you, it's a hugely diverse sport – from the 100-metre sprint to the 100-mile desert ultra-marathon. It is also an integral component of many other sports, such as football, rugby and field hockey.

There are, however, some risks associated with running. Numerous studies show that a high percentage of both novice and professional runners experience pain or injuries as a direct result of the miles they clock up. It's not uncommon for the runners I work with in my Strength & Conditioning gym to believe that getting injured during their career is a certainty.

All physical training places stress on the body. Stress causes adaptation, which in turn improves performance, this is *positive stress*. Physical stress should not, however, be confused with injury. Negative or *maladaptive stress* results in physical regressions and injury. Runners mainly get injured when they haven't developed enough strength and endurance to cope with the stresses that running places on their bodies.

In this book, I will teach you to effectively activate, mobilise, and strengthen the muscles (while building endurance) to support your structure. Not only will this reduce your risk of injury, it will greatly improve your running performance.

Get the Video

The videos to accompany each exercise are available to download for free from **http://geni.us/runners** Simply enrol in the course and you'll have free access to all 28 videos.

http://geni.us/runners

If you type above link into a browser, please note that there is no "www."

Chapter One: Posture, Breathing & Running Mechanics

• Posture

Good posture aligns your body and reduces the stress placed on the joints and supporting muscles, tendons and ligaments by the impact of daily life. It allows maximum movement efficiency, which decreases joint stress, increases overall performance, and optimises the function of your internal organs and nervous system.

Posture does not just relate to how you stand or sit. It is also dynamic and applies to movements such as bending over, squatting, or running. Good posture is essential for running performance.

Ultimately, when it comes to running, most emphasis is placed on your legs and core. However, if you have rounded shoulders and a forward head posture, it will restrict your running efficiency (just try taking a deep breath in this position).

Below are three exercises to help you to regain/maintain good upper-body posture and shoulder health.

• Band Front-to-Backs

The band front-to-back is a great mobility drill for your shoulders.

The front-to-back motion mobilises all the muscles that restrict shoulder retraction (moving the shoulder blades backwards) and overhead positions, such as your pecs (chest).

1. Grab a red band with a wide, over-hand grip. The wider your arms, the easier it is to move the band overhead and down towards your glutes.

2. The band allows you the freedom to widen your grip as you pass it overhead. Your grip should be wide enough so that you aren't forced to aggressively stretch the band out as you perform the movement, as this can cause you to shrug your shoulders, engaging musculature rather than promoting mobility.

3. Start with the band at your hips and, maintaining straight arms throughout, pass it overhead until it reaches your glutes, or the range of motion you can achieve.

4. Complete 2-4 sets of 5-10 reps.

• Band Pull-Aparts

As a strength and conditioning coach who works with athletes and the general public, I can't overstate how effective band pull-apart variations are at restoring and maintaining shoulder health. Every client I have prescribed these to has had amazing results.

Band pull-apart variations are especially great for lifters, but anyone looking to improve their upper-body posture and shoulder health will benefit from them.

During these exercises avoid shoulder shrugging, as this brings your upper traps into play. You want to work the musculature of the upper back that is responsible for shoulder retraction, not elevation.

1. Use a yellow or red long band. The tension can be varied by taking a wider or narrower grip.

2. Take an over-hand grip (palms facing down) on the band and place your arms out in front of you with your elbows straight. Grip the band at shoulder width if you can.

3. With your arms straight, pull your arms outwards, so the band stretches and comes to your mid chest.

4. The band can also be pulled to your abdomen, forehead or diagonally. This varies the angle at which your shoulders are working.

5. Don't allow the band to jerk you back to the starting position. Keep it under control throughout the whole movement.

6. Complete 2-4 sets of 10-20 reps.

• Band Face-Pulls

Face-pulls are one of the best exercises to rehabilitate and develop your upper back and shoulders.

Resistance bands apply *accommodating resistance*. This means that the resistance increases as you progress through the exercise and helps to maximise muscle contraction. As you get to the top of the face-pull, your rear delts, traps and rhomboids must increase their engagement to overcome the extra resistance as the band tension increases.

1. Use a yellow or red band. You can alter the tension by standing closer or further away from the band attachment point.

2. Attach the band to something solid at chest height, either looping the band around and holding both ends, or looping the band through itself so you have hold of one end of the band with both hands.

3. Facing the attachment point, grab the band with an over-hand grip. Or, you can grasp the band with just your fingers, rather than a full grip, to help encourage the upper back to work as the primary mover rather than the biceps.

4. Step backwards to apply tension to the band.

5. Keep your chin back.

6. Pull backwards and slightly upward to bring yourself into a double bicep pose position. Maintain good head posture, pull your hands back to your temples and don't push your head towards the band.

7. Ensure you consciously engage your upper back and rear delts, rather than just pulling with your biceps. Visualise the muscle you are working to increase its engagement and build *mind-muscle connection*.

8. Return to the starting position under control, allowing your shoulders to extend slightly.

9. Complete 2-4 sets of 10-20 reps.

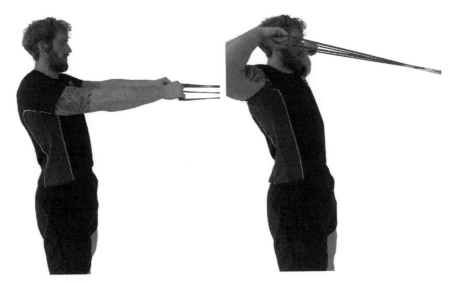

• Breathing

It's important to breathe deeply through your belly using your diaphragm. This pulls your diaphragm down, expands your lungs, and consequently allows you to take in more oxygen.

The Diaphragm

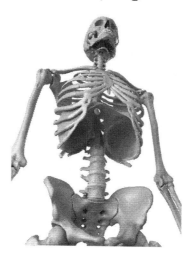

To practise diaphragmatic breathing, place one hand on your chest and one on your belly. Imagine a balloon low in your stomach. As you inhale through your nose or mouth the balloon expands, and as you exhale through your mouth it deflates. If your chest raises instead of your belly your breathing is too shallow and you won't take in as much oxygen.

Many people breathe through the top of their chest, especially when mouth-breathing. This causes muscles that are not designed for respiration to over work, and creates excess tension in unforeseen places, such as the neck muscles. Breathing at the top of the chest can also weaken the diaphragm through underuse and can result in fatigue during exercise and a performance reduction.

Nasal breathing increases rib cage and diaphragm engagement during inhalation. This is beneficial because it drives more oxygen into the lower lobes of your lungs compared to mouth breathing. However, nasal breathing may not allow you to draw in enough oxygen when working at a high intensity. Whether you use nasal or mouth breathing, the important thing is to maintain a constant rhythm, rather than randomly mixing the two.

While many experts agree that mouth breathing is the best way to take in oxygen at high intensities, if you can use nasal breathing while working at low-moderate intensities, I recommend you do so.

Nasal breathing has also been shown to bring the heart and breath rate down more quickly during recovery.

Here's one way to work on your breathing during your next running session.

- Drive your chest up and your shoulders back. Imagine you are trying to look over a fence that is an inch too high, without going up onto your toes; look forward, not down.

- Breathe deeply through your nose or mouth while engaging your diaphragm (as described above), before exhaling through your mouth.

Find the right breathing strategy for you and allow it to work in synchronization with your movements. For example, you may inhale for two strides and out for two.

• Breathing for Resistance Training

Often it is effective to use *anatomical breathing*. Anatomical breathing synchronises your breath to match the movement of the exercise. For example, during a kettlebell swing, you would normally exhale in the bending phase when your ribcage and stomach are compressed, and inhale when you are in an upright position where your ribcage is elevated.

Anatomical breathing is effective while running and working with moderate loads. However, this book focuses on resistance training, and for this sort of training, it often it makes more sense to use a breathing strategy that creates greater tension in your trunk. This tension minimises the risk of injury and maximises performance, and is often referred to as *biomechanical breathing*.

During biomechanical breathing, the athlete matches their inhalation with the downward (eccentric) phase of the exercise and their exhalation with the upward (concentric) phase. They normally exhale during the latter stage of the upward phase.

Biomechanical breathing is normally coupled with the use of the Valsalva manoeuvre. This is "a moderately forceful attempted exhalation against a closed airway" (like equalizing your ears on an airplane by blowing against a pinched nose).

This manoeuvre, combined with a braced core, creates intra-abdominal pressure (IAP) and stabilises the spine. To visualise this, imagine the rigidity of a sealed plastic bottle full of air, compared to that of an open bottle.

Biomechanical breathing is an effective strategy. We can take this further by inhaling before starting the exercise and exhaling on completion. This, combined with the Valsalva manoeuvre, can cause a rise in blood pressure and dizziness. However, the performance benefits and reduced risk of injury generally outweigh the risks, barring other health considerations.

• Running Mechanics

Walking and running are basic aspects of human movement and should be something that you do daily. Ironically, they are the most intricate movement patterns to explain in detail.

It's often mistakenly believed that people inherently run with correct form. In reality, muscular imbalances and weaknesses mean that many people have poor running mechanics. This is often compounded by a lack of awareness of the correct form.

In this section, I will assume that you have no underlying issues and that you also wear suitable footwear (poor footwear is a cause of many problems). This section does not include a gait analysis – that can't be done in a book! – instead I will teach you the guidelines for developing optimal form while running.

An individual has a unique, distinctive gait; often it is easy to identify a friend simply by the way they walk and run. When developing your own running technique, it is key to work with your body, not against it. Just because a world class marathon runner runs in a certain way, it doesn't necessarily mean you should mimic their style.

There is, however, professional consensus on "correct" running technique, and you will benefit by observing the best athletes and coaches and adapting your style accordingly. However, if you have run in a particular way all your life, changing your style suddenly can result in structural stresses and injuries. So, take your time and implement changes gradually.

The following guidelines are considered "best practice" when developing a solid running technique.

Good upper-body posture should be maintained while running, but the torso should tilt forward slightly, driving your weight forward with your chest.

Your arms should be bent at 90 degrees or less, with your hands in a relaxed fist. This results in your rear hand coming in line with your hips or slightly higher, and your front arm coming up to your chest. Your arms should swing towards the centre of your body (the midline), but not cross it or punch forward as this can throw you off balance.

As your right leg strides forward, your left arm should swing forward. This not only keeps you balanced, but also creates a diagonal stretch across your front (from right shoulder to left hip), creating elastic energy that when released helps to propel your next stride.

The height at the front and back of the swing will depend on your speed. When sprinting, runners will often bring their front hand up to their face, usually with an open hand (for aerodynamics). However, when covering longer distances, more emphasis is placed on relaxation and balance, rather than forward drive.

Running form for both sprinters and distance runners is actually very similar. A sprinter's foot will tend to strike down closer to their centre of mass (under their hips), whereas a distance runner's foot will strike a little further forward. But in both cases, the striding foot should land *directly* under the knee.

If your foot lands *in front* of your knee:

- It creates a strong braking force that slows you down, and causes unnecessary impact and strain to the lower leg.

- There is more ground contact time, which also slows you down.

- Cadence (stride frequency) will reduce as a symptom of over-striding.

Foot strike, which refers to how and where your foot first hits the ground (heel, midfoot or forefoot), is an aspect of running that has become a real bone of contention.

Jump up and down on the spot for a few seconds and you will quickly feel that landing on the midfoot is the most effective way to reduce impact while maximising elastic energy (springiness).

This is a strong argument in favour of midfoot striking, but be careful, as attempting to change your foot strike over a short period of time can lead to injury.

Running should feel natural, so start by working on the bullet points below:

- Maintain good upper body posture with a slight forward tilt of your torso.

- Bend your arms at 90 degrees or less, swinging them forward and back to maintain forward drive and balance. Your torso will naturally rotate slightly as you run, so you don't want to overemphasise this by allowing your arms to cross your midline.

- Breathe deeply using your diaphragm and try to regulate your breathing with your strides.

- Land your striding foot directly under your knee.

- Run smoothly, and make a conscious effort to strike the floor softly. Push up and off the floor behind you to propel yourself forward. Aim to bring your rear shin to above knee height.

Chapter Two: Activation & Mobilisation

• Introduction

When it comes to performance and structural health, there needs to be a balance between rigidity and mobility.

Too much rigidity will result in a reduced range of motion of the associated joints. This not only limits your ability to move well, but also makes each movement more taxing. If there is too much mobility, the associated joints risk injury as they are unsupported by the surrounding structures.

Mobility is often overemphasised for injury prevention and structural health. Yes, we want to mobilise our joints to relieve tension and allow good movement. However, our joints also need rigidity to handle the stresses placed on them.

In this chapter, I will show you how to mobilise and activate the muscles commonly affected by running to keep your tissues in good health.

It's important to note that if a muscle is chronically tight, stretching it may not be enough to solve the problem. The hamstrings are a good example; they often become tight to compensate for a lack of core stability or because your glutes (buttock muscles) aren't pulling their weight.

Stretching a tight muscle is usually an effective part of a complete solution, along with activation and strengthening of associated muscles to rectify any underlying issues.

• Activation

Activation refers to getting a specific muscle working.

Simply put, some muscles may not pull their weight and will often benefit from extra exercises to help get them *firing* (contracting) as they should. If one muscle doesn't fire properly, it causes other muscles to over-compensate.

A common example is when the glutes don't fire, so other muscles must pick up the slack. This causes a wide variety of issues and ultimately reduces performance.

This section contains six activation drills that are effective exercises to perform prior to your run and can even be used as light training (active recovery) in between running sessions.

Active recovery is the act of performing low-intensity exercises to aid recovery. Your blood carries nutrients that are vital for recovery, so gently increasing circulation will speed up the process.

If you suffer from delayed onset muscle soreness (DOMS) days after a workout, light walking or jogging may help to relieve it.

• Banded Glute Bridges

Banded glute bridges can be performed without a band, although placing one around your knees and driving them apart (abducting your legs), really helps to maximise glute engagement as you extend your hips up from the floor.

This exercise specifically targets the main buttock muscle (technical name: *gluteus maximus*, illustrated below), which is responsible for extending your hips. Hip extension is your driving force when running, so the development of your glutes and hamstrings (hip extensors) is important.

The Gluteus Maximus

1. Sit on the floor and place a small band around your legs, just above your knees.

2. Lie back, so your head is flat to the floor.

3. Place your hands to the side.

4. Bend your knees and bring your heels towards your glutes. This prevents your hamstrings from taking over the work.

5. Place your feet flat to the floor, either together or hip-width apart.

6. Spread your knees apart to abduct and externally rotate your hips.

7. Squeeze your glutes and extend your hips.

8. Hold at the top for 2-3 seconds before returning to the starting position.

9. Complete 3-5 sets of 20-30 reps.

Above is the standard glute bridge set up. However, there are a few slight changes that can be made to help increase glute engagement.

Give them a go and see what works for you.

1. Tilt your pelvis by bringing your lower back flat to the floor.

2. Flex your head slightly, bringing your chin to your chest, rather than keeping it flat to the floor.

3. Come up onto your heels and take your toes off the floor.

4. Rather than having your palms flat to the floor, bend your elbows, clench your fists, and drive your arms into the floor.

• Banded Lateral Walks

Lateral band walks are a superb exercise to strengthen and build endurance in your *gluteus medius*. This muscle is responsible for stabilising you while you're on one leg.

If the *gluteus medius* is not pulling its weight, other muscles must compensate and this can often lead to injuries. It is extremely beneficial to strengthen and build endurance in this muscle.

The Gluteus Medius

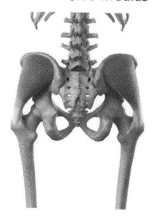

This drill can be done with a short band placed just above or below your knees, with a long band in a figure X, or looping the whole band under the arches of your feet (my personal favourite).

1. Take a long band and hold it at either end in each hand.

2. Loop the band under the arches of your feet.

3. Stand up tall with good posture, bend your knees slightly.

4. Step 1-2 foot-lengths to the right. Stay in control and don't allow your leg to be dragged by the band.

5. Complete 3-5 sets of 10-20 strides in each direction.

• Banded Psoas March

While it is common to need to activate and strengthen the glutes, the hip flexors are the opposite and normally need to be mobilised.

Prolonged sitting is often a huge factor. Sitting weakens your glutes through underuse, while your hip flexors are held flexed which often causes them to tighten and become tense.

It's easy to see how keeping your hip flexors in a shortened position for extended periods can cause issues. However, an area that often becomes underused (even while running) is the full range of hip flexion. This is the act of moving your hip beyond the 90-degree angle that a seated position keeps you in.

It's important to work your hip flexors through full flexion and extension to promote proper function as weak muscles often become tense.

1. Sit on the floor and place the band around the centre of your feet.

2. Lie back, so your head is flat on the floor.

3. Bend your knees and raise your feet up, bringing your legs right back towards your torso.

4. Slowly extend your left leg, while ensuring your right leg remains in a fully flexed position.

5. Slowly return your left leg back to a flexed position and proceed to extend your right leg.

6. Complete 3-5 sets of 10-20 reps (counting each leg extension as a rep).

• Terminal Knee Extensions

Terminal knee extensions are ideal to get the quads (specifically, the inner quad muscle, the *vastus medialis*), warmed up. This muscle is responsible for stabilising your knee cap (*patella*).

For those who suffer with patella tendon issues, the following exercise is an awesome rehab drill. It places low stress on the soft tissues supporting the knee, while simultaneously working the supporting muscles intensely.

Of the quads, the central thigh muscle (*rectus femoris*) is the most commonly strained. However, it's important to consider all the quad muscles when it comes to structural health.

The *rectus femoris* and the quad muscle on the outer side of your thigh (*vastus lateralis*) apply lateral forces on the knee cap. It is important to help balance this force by strengthening the *vastus medialis*.

The Vastus Medialis

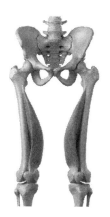

1. Place a medium-to-high tension band around something solid at knee height.

2. Step into the band with one leg and place the band around the back of the knee (in the crease).

3. Step back to apply tension to the band.

4. With the leg that is attached to the band, slowly roll forward onto the ball of the foot to bend your knee.

5. Slowly bring your foot back down onto your heel and lock your knee fully, ensuring you don't place unnecessary stress on the joint by forcing it into a hyperextension.

6. Complete 3-4 sets of 15-20 reps on each side.

• Banded Stability Complex – Iso Hold, Single Leg Romanian Deadlift, & Skater Squat

This exercise can be broken down into three individual sections, but works well as a sequence of exercises joined together.

Performing single leg Romanian deadlifts and skater squats on one leg improves stability. The band attached to the leg makes the exercise more challenging and beneficial, especially when the band tension pulls your knee inwards (*valgus*).

I'll come back to the Romanian deadlift as a strength exercise later in the book; for now, the focus is on stability.

1. Place a low-tension band around something solid at knee height.

2. Step into the band with your right leg while your left side is closest to the band attachment point. This results in the band tension pulling you into *valgus* (you are resisting).

3. Step away from the attachment point to apply tension to the band.

4. Raise your left leg off the ground.

5. Begin by performing an isometric hold (no change in muscle length) for 15-20 seconds.

6. Perform 5-10 single leg Romanian deadlifts: with a slight bend of your knee, push your glutes rearwards so your hips bend, and your torso drops forward.

7. Perform 5-10 skater squats: single leg squat with your non-supporting leg to the rear. Increase depth gradually, ensuring your knee doesn't track too far forward.

8. Complete 2-3 sets of this complex on each side

• Single Leg Swap

The single leg swap is an awesome proprioception drill. It builds fantastic foot and ankle stability, as well as being a great stabiliser for your core.

While standing on one leg, pass a weight across your body. The shift of weight will exert force on your foot and knee. The idea is to resist these forces.

Proprioception is the body's ability to transmit a sense of position to the spinal cord/brain, analyse that information and react to it. For example, touching your nose with your eyes closed. Proprioception effects balance, coordination and agility.

Proprioception is vital to injury prevention. For example, if your ankle begins to roll outwards, receptors called muscle spindles in your peroneal muscles will detect the change of length (stretch) and stimulate a contraction of the muscle to prevent injury to the ankle.

The Peroneus Longus   **The Peroneus Brevis**

A dumbbell can be used, but a kettlebell works best.

1. Pick up a kettlebell and hold it in your right hand.

2. Stand on one leg, raising the leg to the front.

3. Slowly pass the kettlebell from your right hand to your left hand. Hold it steady in your left hand at your side for second, before passing it back across to your right hand.

4. Keep your core braced throughout. Don't lean to the opposite side as you pass the kettlebell across.

5. Complete 2-3 sets of 10 passes on each leg.

• Mobility

Due to the number of miles most runners cover, it is essential to maintain the health of your soft tissue through foam-rolling and stretching. This chapter teaches you drills that will release and stretch these muscles.

Fascia are the sheets of connective tissue beneath the skin that attach, stabilise, enclose and separate muscles and other internal organs. It's been proven that muscle fascia plays a major role in muscle tension.

The self-myofascial release techniques shown in this book are a hands-on therapy that you can perform on yourself, with a foam roller or massage ball. These techniques use pressure to stimulate a sensory receptor called the *Golgi* tendon organ that tells the muscle fibres to relax.

These techniques will *not* stimulate a long-term change in muscle tension by themselves. Instead they will cause a short-term release of muscle tension, which in turn will allow you to gain a more effective stretch to the tissues.

Release techniques and stretching will provide you with short-term relief from excessive tension that might cause pain, discomfort or even limit performance. The long-term aim is to combine these techniques with exercises that strengthen specific muscles and develop optimal running mechanics and soft tissue health.

It's all about finding the right balance between mobility and rigidity. Mobility is the best place to start, because good mobility will allow you to effectively perform the exercises that increase your strength and joint rigidity.

• Calve Release Techniques & Stretches

The calves are made up of two major muscles: the *gastrocnemius* and the *soleus*. Both attach to the heel via the *Achilles* tendon and when they contract they raise your heels off the floor. These muscles are integral to walking and running, and become stressed due to their high workload. Rolling and stretching the soft tissues is highly beneficial.

It isn't necessary to spend hours rolling every part of your body, but certain areas respond well to myofascial release and the calve group is one of them.

You can also roll the outsides of your lower leg while working the calves. This targets your *peroneus* group, which can also become tense, especially when your ankle stability has been heavily challenged – for example when running on uneven surfaces.

The Gastrocnemius   The Soleus

• Release Technique

Foam Rolling:

1. Sit on the floor and place a foam roller under the top of your calf.

2. Both sides can be done at the same time if the roller is long enough, but doing one at a time allows for more pressure to be placed through the calves.

3. If rolling your right leg, place your left foot over your right, then raise your body up with your hands.

4. Slowly roll up and down the muscle for 30-60 seconds. Ensure you don't roll over the back of the knee, as there are structures in your knee crease that you don't respond well to rolling. Focus on the bulk of the muscle.

5. Complete 1-2 times on each side.

• Stretches

If you stretch your calves with a straight knee, the stretch will target mainly the gastrocnemius. Bent knees will transfer the stretch onto the soleus.

You can perform a quick calve stretch by placing one foot forward on its heel and sitting back to create a stretch. Using a small platform is the most effective way to target the area.

1. Stand with the balls of your feet on the edge of a step or platform.

2. Both legs can be stretched at once, or you can raise one leg up to apply more weight to the supporting leg and increase the stretch.

3. When stretching the gastroc, keep your knee(s) straight.

4. You can also change the angle at which your toes are pointing to vary the stretch.

5. Bend you knee(s) slightly and you will feel the stretch transition from your gastroc to your soleus.

6. Repeat on both sides if stretching each leg independently.

7. Hold for 30-60 seconds, or for 2 minutes if the musculature is very tense.

8. Complete 1-3 sets.

• Hamstring Release Techniques & Stretches

It's common for a runner's hamstrings to become tight and for strains to occur.

Tightness can be down to muscular imbalances where the glutes are weak, or the quads are stronger than the hamstrings. It is often a case of performing maintenance work to help alleviate tension that's been built up from all your mileage.

If your hamstrings are excessively tight they can pull your pelvis into a posterior tilt, which in turn can flatten your lower back and cause pain. In these cases, hamstring stretches will be beneficial.

It's important to understand that your hamstrings could be tense because your pelvis has an anterior (forward) tilt, which pulls your hamstrings upwards. In this case, the muscle can be in a lengthened state while also being tense (this is counter-intuitive for many people, because they equate "lengthened" with "stretched" which is not always the case).

In these circumstances, stretching is not the best solution. Instead, strengthening the hamstrings (along with the glutes and abs), is the best approach, especially when combined with stretching the muscles that are pulling the pelvis into an anterior tilt, such as the hip flexors.

The hamstrings are a good example of a muscle being chronically tight – not because of an issue with the hamstrings, but because of a lack of core stability. Sometimes this is also caused when the glutes aren't pulling their weight and the hamstrings tighten to compensate.

This goes to show that stretching a muscle that is tight is not always the solution on its own, but can be an effective part of a complete solution.

• Release Techniques

Foam Rolling:

1. Sit on the floor and place a foam roller under the top of your right or left hamstring.

2. Both sides can be done at the same time if the roller is long enough. However, doing one at a time allows for more pressure to be placed through the hamstrings.

3. If rolling your right leg, place your left foot over your right, then raise yourself up with your hands.

4. Slowly roll up and down the muscle for 30-60 seconds. Ensure you don't roll over the back of the knee, as there are structures in your knee crease (lymph nodes) that you don't want to drive a roller into. Focus on the bulk of the muscle.

5. Complete 1-2 times on each side.

High Hamstring Release Technique:

A massage ball can be used to roll throughout the entire length of the hamstrings. However, this drill is designed specifically to reach the top of your hamstrings.

This can be specifically beneficial for those who have an anterior pelvic tilt, which pulls the hamstrings upwards causing excessive tension in the upper hamstrings.

1. Place the massage ball on a solid chair or platform.

2. Sit on the ball so that it is driven into the top of your hamstrings.

3. Knead the soft tissue and find any areas of excessive tension.

4. Apply pressure to an area of tension and slowly straighten and bend the knee.

5. Complete 1-2 sets of 5-10 reps on each leg.

• Stretches

Standing Bilateral Stretch:

It's important to understand that rounding your spine and dropping down to touch your toes isn't necessarily a true test of hamstring flexibility. You might have a mobile lower spine that allows you to bend over double.

1. Stand with your feet shoulder-width or slightly wider apart.

2. Keep your knees straight throughout. They don't, however, have to be locked out – you can maintain a soft knee position.

3. Hinge at your hips by driving your glutes back, ensuring your knees don't bend and your chest remains proud.

4. As your glutes move back, you will feel the stretch on your hamstrings.

5. Hold for 30-60 seconds, or for 2 minutes if the musculature is very tense.

6. Complete 1-3 times.

Seated Unilateral Stretch:

Here's an excellent stretch that can be done whilst sat at your desk.

1. Sit at the front of your chair.

2. Place your right leg straight out onto your heel.

3. Shift your glutes back slightly, tilting your pelvis forward. Do this correctly and you will feel the stretch in your hamstring.

4. Lean forward with your torso, ensuring you don't round your back.

5. Hold for 30-60 seconds, or for 2 minutes if the musculature is very tense.

6. Complete 1-3 times on each side.

A similar stretch can be done while standing, pictured below.

Lying Band Stretch:

Bands can be used effectively during many stretches.

1. Sit on the floor.

2. Place the resistance band around the arch of one foot, holding it with both hands.

3. Lie back, so your head is flat to the floor. Maintain a neutral spine position.

4. Pull on the band to raise the leg up to facilitate the stretch.

5. Hold for 30-60 seconds, or for 2 minutes if the musculature is very tense.

6. Complete 1-3 times on each side.

• Adductor Release Techniques & Stretches

The adductors are a large group of muscles on your inner thigh that are responsible for bringing your legs back towards your body from the side. While running, they draw your legs together to control swinging and help to stabilise your stride.

They oppose your hip abductors (gluteal muscles), and it's important that both these groups are balanced. If the adductors are tight, it can inhibit your glutes and create back pain.

The adductors often get neglected when training; some women don't want to develop their inner thighs and men generally pay more attention to their quads, calves and hamstrings.

The Adductor Magnus – One of the Adductors

• Release Techniques

Foam Rolling:

When rolling, it's important to ensure that you try to cover the full length of the muscle. However, muscles will often cross joints and areas which don't react well to having pressure placed on them. This can be due to the presence of things like neurovascular bundles – combinations of nerves, arteries, veins and lymphatic vessels that travel together in the body.

Your groin is one area where caution must be practised. However, you can still roll throughout the length of the adductors effectively.

1. Lie face down on the floor with the roller to your side, at your hips.

2. Raise the leg you are rolling out to the side and place your inner thigh on the roller.

3. If you can't raise your leg to the roller, simply lower it down, ensuring the roller ends up perpendicular to your leg.

4. Use your forearms to raise your body up to apply more pressure onto the foam roller.

5. Slowly roll up and down the muscle mass for 30-60 seconds.

6. Complete 1-2 times on each side.

Barbell Release Technique:

Foam rolling often requires you to hold yourself in taxing positions as you roll the targeted muscle(s). However, the weight of a barbell can be used to effectively roll muscles targeted while sitting.

This is an awesome technique to target your adductors and inner quad muscles.

1. Sit on the floor and place your left leg out to the side.

2. Place the sleeve of the barbell onto your inner thigh.

3. Slowly roll up and down the muscle mass for 30-60 seconds.

4. Complete 1-2 times on each side.

• Stretches

Seated Butterfly Stretch:

This is a simple but effective stretch for your adductors.

1. Sit on the floor and place the soles of your feet together.

2. Pull your heels in towards your groin.

3. Hold onto the balls of your feet.

4. Lean forward with your torso, keeping your spine straight, and push your knees towards the ground.

5. Hold for 30-60 seconds, or for 2 minutes if the musculature is very tense.

6. Complete 1-3 times on each side.

Deep Squat Stretch:

This is my favourite stretch for your lower body, as it targets every muscle essential for achieving a deep squat.

I recommend spending as much time as you can in a deep squat. Some experts prescribe at least 10 minutes a day.

1. Stand with your feet shoulder-width apart. Toes can be angled out slightly (anywhere up to around 30 degrees).

2. Squat down into the deepest squat you can achieve. Try to maintain a neutral spine with a proud chest.

3. Some lumbar flexion (where your lower back rounds slightly as your pelvis tilts underneath) in a deep squat is normal, just ensure it is not excessive or putting stress on your lower back.

4. Place your hands into a prayer position and use your elbows to push your knees outwards.

5. Hold for 30-60 seconds, or for 2 minutes if the musculature is very tense.

6. Complete 1-3 times on each side.

• Hip Flexors & Quadriceps Release Techniques & Stretches

Your hip flexors do exactly what you'd expect: flex your hips! They play a huge role in running and can easily become tense when overworked.

Prolonged sitting places your hip flexors in a shortened position. This reinforces the need for hip flexor mobility exercises, since we tend to spend more time than we should in seated positions.

Since one of the hip flexors (*psoas major*) originates on your lower spine and the other originates on your pelvis (*iliacus*), they can pull on your lower spine, putting your hips into an anterior tilt, often resulting in back pain.

Your *quadriceps* (thighs) can also play a role with tightness in this area, as one of the quads also acts as a hip flexor (*rectus femoris*).

The quads often become tight as they engage heavily during physical activities such as squatting, jumping and running. As mentioned previously, if the quads become much stronger than the hamstrings and glutes, it can increase your risk of hamstring strains and cause postural issues that result in back pain.

The Iliacus: One of the hip flexors	The Psoas Major: One of the hip flexors	The Rectus Femoris: A quadricep muscle that also acts as a hip flexor
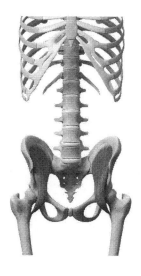	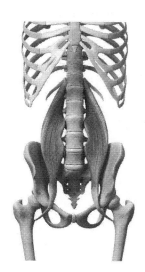	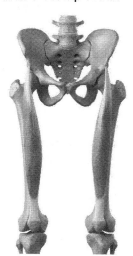

• Release Techniques

Foam Roller or Massage Ball:

The deep origin of the hip flexors mean that you won't get a lot of self-myofascial release to the area. However, you can target some of the more superficial tissue that crosses your hip joint.

Use the same position to foam roll right down to your knee to release your quads.

1. Place the foam roller or massage ball on the floor.

2. Lay onto the roller at the crease of your hip on one side. Practise caution when placing a massage ball into the crease of the hip or groin area, to not overly stress the area.

3. Slowly roll up and down the muscle mass for 30-60 seconds.

4. Complete 1-2 sets on each side.

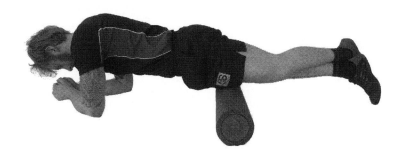

• Stretches

Kneeling:

This stretch is predominantly aimed at the hip flexors, but will also target the quads. The hip flexors and quads are easy to stretch. However, individuals often adopt a position that throws their pelvis into an anterior tilt. This can exacerbate any low back pain they may be suffering from. It's far more effective to keep your pelvis in a neutral position while squeezing your glutes.

We can often get one muscle set to relax by squeezing an opposing muscle set (known as *reciprocal inhibition*). Contracting the glutes helps to facilitate a greater stretch.

1. Adopt a half-kneeling position, with your left knee down and your right foot flat on the floor to the front, with a knee bend of 90 degrees.

2. Squeeze your glutes, focussing on the left side, and drive your left hip forward into hyperextension to facilitate the stretch. Your pelvis should remain neutral throughout.

3. Raising the same arm as the hip flexor you are stretching and reaching over the opposite shoulder really increases the stretch through the hip flexors and the quads.

4. Hold for 30-60 seconds, or for 2 minutes if the musculature is very tense.

5. Complete 1-3 times on each side.

Standing Quadricep Stretch:

This is the most common quad stretch. Again, it will target both the hip flexors and quads, with most emphasis on the quads.

People may argue that you should be able to perform this stretch without having to hold onto a supporting structure and, yes, ideally you should. However, your aim is to stretch your quads, and if you need to hold onto something to facilitate the stretch, do so. If you do struggle standing on one leg, I suggest you add in some balance work to your regime, such as single leg swaps.

1. From a standing position, grasp the top of your right foot with your right hand.

2. Maintain a soft knee position with the supporting leg.

3. Pull your right foot up towards your glutes, keep your right knee next to your left. This ensures you maintain a full stretch down the length of your quads.

4. Squeeze your glutes, focusing on the right side, and drive your right hip forward into hyperextension to facilitate the stretch. Your pelvis should remain neutral throughout.

5. Hold for 30-60 seconds, or for 2 minutes if the musculature is very tense.

6. Complete 1-3 times on each side.

Couch:

The couch stretch is an effective variation that can increase the intensity of both the hip flexor and quad stretch.

The stretch can be done with the leg being stretched up behind you against a wall, or with the upper side of the foot placed on a bench or chair, allowing your knee to rest on the floor or a well-cushioned mat.

1. Place your right leg against a wall, or the top of your foot onto a raised platform that is just below knee height.

2. This places you in a half-kneeling position, with your left foot flat on the floor to the front, with a knee bend of 90 degrees.

3. Squeeze your glutes, specifically the right side, and drive your right hip forward into hyper-extension to facilitate the stretch. Your pelvis should remain neutral.

4. Raising the arm on the side of the stretch and reaching over the opposite shoulder increases the stretch.

5. Hold for 30-60 seconds, or for 2 minutes if the musculature is very tense.

6. Complete 1-3 times on each side.

• Foam Rolling the Thigh

The *tensor fasciae latae* (TFL) is located on the outside of your upper thigh and attaches to the *iliotibial band* (ITB), along with the gluteus maximus.

The ITB is a sheet of fascia which runs down your outer thigh from your hip to just below your knee and, along with the muscles that connect into it, plays a role in stabilising your hip and knee.

The Tensor Fasciae Latae (TFL)

When experiencing pain, it's a common fault for people to immediately zone in on the specific area of discomfort. Often, the problem results from other areas of tension or imbalance. It's usually worthwhile to consider the areas directly above and below, or either side the site of pain. Rolling the ITB may alleviate some outer leg pain, but it is not the solution to all issues in this area.

Discomfort on the outer side of your leg can be helped by strengthening your leg's supporting muscles, such as your *gluteus medius*, and releasing the muscles that can take up the slack when the glutes are not working efficiently, such as the TFL.

Rolling the TFL helps to relieve tension, which in turn helps to keep the ITB in good health. This is not the solution to all your problems, but can be an effective part of your mobility regime.

1. Lie on the foam roller with the outer side of your left hip, directly where your pants pocket would be.

2. Bring your right leg in front of your left and place your foot down in line with your left knee for support.

3. Use your left forearm and right hand to support yourself.

4. Use your arms and right leg to raise your body up to apply more pressure onto the foam roller.

5. Slowly roll up and down the muscle for 30-60 Seconds.

6. Repeat on both sides.

7. Complete 1-2 sets on each side.

• Glute Release Techniques & Stretches

The three muscles of the glutes are an area that needs extra attention when it comes to strength. They can often become tense and cause pain in your low back and hamstrings.

The *piriformis* is a small muscle located under your glutes. The sciatic nerve travels either underneath or through the piriformis.

The piriformis often becomes stressed through overwork while running, especially if your main gluteal muscles don't fire as well as they should.

When the piriformis becomes stressed, it can be a literal pain in your butt, and due to the location of your sciatic nerve can result in sciatic pain that shoots down the leg from the lower back.

The Gluteus Maximus

The Piriformis

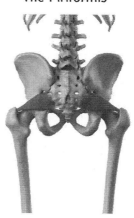

• Release Techniques

Foam Roller or Massage Ball:

You must be very careful with the glutes when attempting self-myofascial release because of the location of the sciatic nerve which passes through the gluteal area and down your leg.

Driving a massage ball into your sciatic nerve can potentially leave you with worse symptoms than those you are trying to relieve. It is essential that you target the musculature on the upper gluteal area only.

I do not recommend using release techniques on this area if you are suffering from sciatic pain, or are not certain how you can safely manipulate the soft tissues.

1. Place a foam roller or massage ball on the floor. A foam roller will help to distribute the pressure across the gluteal area and so will be less intense.

2. Place your upper gluteal area on the foam roller (where your back pockets would be).

3. To roll your right-hand side, place your right leg over your left, so the ankle of your right leg is just above your left knee. This lengthens the musculature being worked.

4. If this is not possible, simply drop your right knee off to the side.

5. Slowly roll up and down the muscle mass for 30-60 seconds.

6. Complete 1-2 times on each side.

• Stretches

Seated:

This stretch for your glutes and piriformis can easily be done at your desk.

1. Sit upright in your chair. Don't do this on a chair with wheels.

2. To stretch your right side, place your right leg over your left, so the ankle of your right leg is just above your left knee.

3. Keeping your chest proud, lean towards your right knee. Don't round your spine and bend your head down towards your knee, push your chest forward with a neutral spine.

4. Hold for 30-60 seconds, or for 2 minutes if the musculature is very tense.

5. Complete 1-3 times on each side.

Figure Four:

1. Lie on your back.

2. To stretch your right side, raise your left leg up with your knee bent at 90 degrees.

3. Place your right leg over your left, so the ankle of your right leg is just below your left knee.

4. Reach through and grab round the back of your left leg with both hand and pull towards your chest.

5. Hold for 30-60 seconds, or for 2 minutes if the musculature is very tense.

6. Complete 1-3 times on each side.

Pigeon Stretch:

1. Start on all fours.

2. To stretch your right side, place the outer side of your right leg onto the floor. The sole of your right foot will be pointing to the left, while your knee is pointing to the right.

3. Slide your left leg back as you move your right leg into position.

4. Keep your hips forward-facing and your chest proud, driving your chest upwards to increase the stretch.

5. If you can, keep your right foot in line with your right knee. However, you might need to pull your foot back towards your hip.

6. Hold for 30-60 seconds, or for 2 minutes if the musculature is very tense.

7. Complete 1-3 times on each side.

• Low Back Release Techniques & Stretches

The muscles of the lower back can easily become tense and cause lower back pain.

A major culprit of this pain is often the *quadratus lumborum* (QL) and/or lower *erector spinae*. These muscles are located on either side of the spine and attach to your pelvis, so any imbalances here can cause postural issues and have negative effects on your whole body.

I don't recommend rolling the lower back with a foam roller. Unlike the thoracic spine, the lumbar spine is not surrounded by other skeletal structures such as your rib cage and shoulder blades, which help support the area.

Although the thoracic spine can benefit from extension drills on the roller, your lumbar spine may not. Often driving a roller into your lower spine will simply cause your back muscles to tighten as they try to protect it.

I prefer to work each side of the spine independently with a massage ball, either laying on it, or placing it on a wall or a door frame.

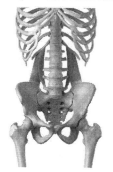
The Quadratus Lumborum

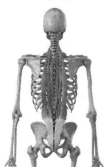
The Erector Spinae

• Release Techniques

Massage Ball:

You can buy massage balls that are peanut shaped so you can work both sides of the spine without applying pressure to the vertebra. However, I feel you can get much deeper when using a single massage ball on one side.

1. Place the ball on the floor if lying on it, or against a wall or door frame at hip height.

2. Place the right side of your lower back onto the ball, just above your pelvis.

3. Keep your pelvis neutral or tilted slightly backwards to drive the soft tissue into the ball.

4. If lying, you can raise the knee of the side you are working, to allow you to drive the ball deeper into the soft tissue.

5. If working in a door frame or similar space, you can push against the structure to the front of you to increase the depth.

6. Slowly roll up and down the muscle mass for 30-60 seconds.

7. Complete 1-2 times on each side.

• Stretches

Hip Rolls:

This is a simple exercise that will help to mobilise your lower back.

1. Lie on your back with your head flat to the floor and your arms spread to your sides.

2. Bend your knees, so your soles are flat on the floor.

3. Slowly roll your knees side to side while keeping both arms flat to the floor.

4. Complete 2-3 sets of 10-20 rolls.

A useful stretch you can couple with this exercise is to bring one or both knees to your chest in the lying position. This will stretch your lower back, glutes and hamstrings.

Iron Cross Stretch:

The iron cross stretch mobilises your hips and lower back, and acts as a great warm-up drill.

1. Lie on your back with your head flat to the floor and your arms spread to your sides.

2. While keeping the other leg flat to the floor, slowly raise one leg and bring it towards your opposite hand.

3. Hold this position for 2-3 seconds before returning to the starting position and continuing with the opposite leg.

4. Complete 2-3 sets of 10 reps.

• Upper Back Release Techniques & Stretches

The thoracic spine consists of the twelve vertebrae between the base of your neck and the bottom of your rib cage. When we refer to the thoracic spine in a training environment, we are talking about the muscles that surround it.

The following drills take a holistic approach to the area, targeting the lats, mid-upper erector spinae, rhomboids, lower-mid traps and pecs, and work to mobilise each individual vertebra.

Lack of thoracic mobility can cause neck and lower back pain, as well as shoulder issues.

The back muscles surrounding   The Rhomboids   The Erector Spinae
the Thoracic Spine

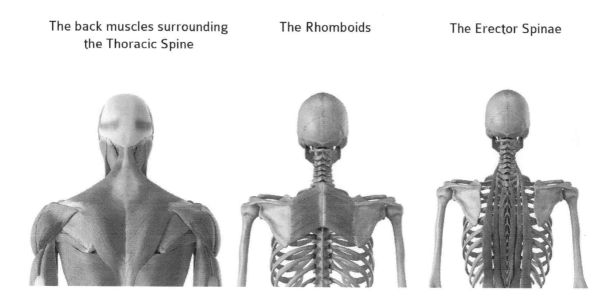

Foam Rolling & Extension Drill:

1. Lie with your mid-back on the foam roller.

2. Extend your arms out in front of you and cross them over each other. You want your shoulders extended to lengthen the muscles of the back.

3. Slowly roll your mid-upper back area up and down for 30-60 seconds.

4. Keep the foam roller static and your arms extended overhead, allowing gravity to do the work and mobilise each vertebra (holding for 30-60 seconds). This is the most effective aspect of foam rolling the thoracic spine.

5. Complete 1-2 times on each side.

Quadruped Thoracic Rotations:

This is a great stretch for mobilising your upper back. However, it can make you feel a little dizzy so take care when standing afterwards.

1. Get down onto all fours.

2. Place your left hand behind your head.

3. Shifting back with your hips facilitates a small degree of lumbar flexion, which will take away the arch. This ensures you don't compensate for the movement by rotating your lumbar spine.

4. Place your left elbow under your torso before rotating round and pointing it towards the ceiling, or as far as your mobility will allow.

5. Follow your elbow with your eyes.

6. Complete 2-3 sets of 5-10 rotations on each side.

Side Lying Thoracic Rotations:

1. Lay on your side.

2. Raise the top leg up to 90 degrees, resting it on a foam roller.

3. Place your hands out to the front in a prayer position.

4. Slowly rotate with your thoracic spine to bring the top arm over, so that the back of your hand touches the floor, or as far as mobility allows.

5. Keep your leg firmly on the foam roller throughout the whole movement.

6. Complete 2-3 sets of 5-10 rotations on each side.

Chapter Three: Core Stability

• Introduction

Your *core* is the musculature of your torso. More specifically, it is the lumbar spine and pelvis, often referred to as your *lumbo-pelvic region* or *lower back*. These muscles are responsible for both stabilisation and the transfer of force from one of movement to the next, for example when changing direction.

The lumbo-pelvic region is at the heart of good movement. If there are any postural issues, muscular imbalances, or weaknesses in this area, problems can arise and manifest themselves from head to toe, especially if you are clocking up the miles. A strong core is essential for runners!

Strength is your ability to exert force and *stability* is your ability to resist force. When we train, we can become very good at exerting force, but the muscles that help us to resist force and stabilise movements can often be neglected.

The primary action of the core is to provide stability, so you must first and foremost train your ability to resist the forces that apply stress to your spine.

While strength is essential for both the function and overall health of your structure, it's not effective to develop the muscles that stabilise your structure in the same way as the *primary mover* muscles that facilitate large/explosive movements.

Large primary movers (lats, quads and pecs, etc.) respond well to high loads, which ultimately stimulate the greatest strength increases. However, the muscles that help to maintain stability require endurance and respond well to isometric holds such as the plank, or high reps with moderate weight. Overloading these assisting muscles with weight will result in primary movers taking over.

Below is a series of strength and conditioning exercises that I use daily to help runners develop their core to develop their overall physical health and performance.

• Birddog

The birddog is a great exercise for working your abs and back and develops both hip and shoulder function.

1. Start on all fours, with your elbows and shoulders over your hands and your hips over your knees.

2. Ensure your spine and pelvis stay neutral. Avoid tipping to one side to compensate.

3. Keep your core tight and slowly extend your right leg behind you, while reaching forward with your left arm to the front (flexing your shoulder). This position can be held like a plank.

4. Return your arm and leg back to the starting position and proceed with the opposite side, or you can bring your left elbow (or palm) to your right knee, before extending them out again without placing them down.

5. Complete 3-5 sets of 10-20 reps (counting each leg extension as a rep).

• McGill Curl Ups

McGill curls ups are named after Dr Stuart McGill. He is a leading spinal researcher who promotes the use of what he refers to as "The Big Three": McGill curl ups, birddogs and side planks. They are his non-negotiable core exercises for a healthy lower spine.

McGill curl ups are essentially a sit up variation, which work your abs without excessively flexing your lumbar vertebra.

The exercise may look easy, but as with all core work, when performed correctly by consciously engaging the muscles you are targeting, they are one of the toughest ab exercises out there.

1. Lie down with your head flat on the floor.

2. Bend your right leg, bringing your heel up towards your glutes, while keeping your left leg extended.

3. Bend your elbows and place your hands under your lower back. This ensures you maintain a neutral spine throughout the movement. Keeping your elbows raised off the floor throughout the movement makes it harder.

4. Slowly raise your head and shoulders up a few inches and maximally contract your abs for 10 seconds, before slowly returning to the starting position.

5. Try not to roll your chin towards your chest. Keep your chin retracted as you raise your shoulders and head up.

6. Complete 3-5 sets of 5 reps with 10 second pauses at the top.

• RKC Plank

Plank variations are isometric holds where your core musculature works to resist gravity as it pushes you into hyperextension and *lateral flexion* (side bending) of your spine.

The key to isometric core exercises is to consciously engage the musculature of the core, including your *transverse abdominis* (TVA).

The TVA is the deepest muscle of the abdominal wall and is an integral component of the core. It is often seen as the body's natural weight lifting belt, and is commonly trained using the *vacuum exercise*.

The vacuum exercise involves drawing your belly button inward toward your spine. Rather than performing this in isolation (which detracts from the rest of the core muscles), we simply retract the stomach slightly to engage the TVA, while bracing our entire core musculature.

Note that during resistance training a lifter will drive their belly outwards slightly (often into a weightlifting belt) while bracing their core. This maximises tension and allows for a greater base of support. However, this technique can take your breath away and is therefore not effective when used for isometrics or circuit training.

The Transverse Abdominis

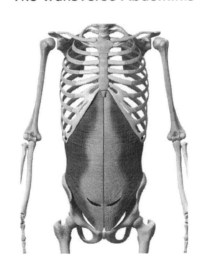

The RKC plank is named after the Russian Kettlebell Challenge by Pavel Tsatsouline, a famous Russian strength coach. It uses a few slight variations from the standard front plank, while concentrating on engaging total body tension.

The RKC plank has been shown to get four times the ab engagement of the conventional front plank, and is my plank variation of choice.

You don't need to hold the RKC for minutes at a time. If you contract your core maximally, short rounds with even shorter rest periods work perfectly.

Often coaches will state that, "If you can plank for a minute with ease, then you need to progress the exercise." I am sure this is true for planks where there is little to no conscious engagement, but if you maximally engage the associated musculature, even 20-30 seconds will be enough for most.

1. Kneel on the floor and clasp your hands together so that your forearms are at a 45-degree angle.

2. Place your forearms onto the floor just as you would during a standard front plank. To increase the intensity, place your arms further forward, so that your elbows sit in front of your shoulders.

3. Step back with your left then right foot at hip to shoulder width.

4. Maximally contract your glutes, which will tilt your pelvis back slightly.

5. Maximally contract your quads and core musculature. Pull back with your forearms to increase your core engagement.

6. Complete 3-5 sets of 30-40 seconds.

• Side Plank

The side plank is an underused exercise that's ideal for the development and maintenance of the deep core musculature that supports your spine and resists lateral flexion (side bending of the spine).

1. Lie on your right-hand side and place your right forearm onto the floor, perpendicular to your body.

2. Placing your left foot on the front of your right foot helps to keep your hips in a balanced position and allows you to easily transition between front and side plank variations.

3. Raise your hips so there is no side bending of your spine and so that your lower legs are raised off the floor.

4. Engage your glutes, so your hips are extended. Having slightly bent hips is a common fault.

5. Maximally brace your core musculature, as you would during a RKC plank.

6. Either keep your left arm flat to your body or raise it to the sky.

7. Complete 2-3 sets of 30-40 seconds on each side.

• Pallof Isometric Holds

However, the *pallof isometric hold* is my favourite anti-rotation exercise.

The pallof isometric hold can be performed in various stances while standing or kneeling. These variations should be practised as they help to build lumbo-pelvic stability in different positions.

1. Use a red band. The tension can be varied by standing closer to, or further away from the band attachment point if required.

2. Attach the band to something solid at chest height, looping the band through itself.

3. Grasp the band with both hands and stand side-on to the attachment point, holding your hands at your chest.

4. Sidestep away from the attachment point to add tension to the band.

5. Ensure that your feet, hips and shoulders are forward facing. Don't counter the band tension by turning away from the attachment point.

6. If performing the pallof press, engage your core and press the band to your front, holding it for 2-5 seconds, before returning it to the starting position and proceeding with successive reps.

7. For an isometric hold, press the band out and hold it for 30-40 seconds.

8. Complete 2-3 sets of 5-15 reps or 30-40 seconds on each side.

Chapter Four: Strength Development

• Introduction

When it comes to physical development in any sport, strength plays a massive role and is often the primary goal for Strength & Conditioning coaches to achieve with their clients. If an athlete is strong, sporting actions require less effort and the stresses caused by the activity are more easily handled.

Strength is not just your ability to produce force, it also has a bearing on the robustness of your skeletal system and soft tissue (specifically muscles, tendons and ligaments). Without their ability to accommodate the load or stresses placed on them, sporting development will be slowed by niggles and injuries.

Strength development is beneficial for everyone, although there can be negatives to placing too much emphasis on strength development, so some runners are averse to resistance training.

Runners have two common objections to strength training:

Won't strength training result in unnecessary bulk?

No.

The right kind of strength training will build lean muscle. For a runner with a relatively healthy diet and adequate mileage, two or three specifically designed strength sessions won't lead to excessive development of muscle mass. If it does, you should take up bodybuilding!

Won't strength training slow me down?

No.

If you concentrate excessively on the development of maximal strength (by using heavy loads), then you may build muscle that is not necessarily fit for the purpose of running, and this could slow you down.

However, strength training will only negatively affect your performance when done to an excessive extent. A runner should definitely not prioritise lifting heavy weights. However, physiology clearly shows that some strength training is vital for optimal performance in running.

Without going too deep into anatomy and physiology, our muscles are made from both fast and slow twitch fibres. These muscle fibres are used for different tasks. For example, slow twitch fibres are beneficial for marathon runners and fast twitch fibres are suited for sprinters.

If you are covering a moderate-to-long distance, you want to develop your slow twitch fibres. However, as with most sports, you will benefit if you can effectively recruit both slow and fast twitch fibres. If you are a marathon runner, it is a priority to develop your slow twitch fibres. However, developing your fast twitch fibres will help to increase your speed and make you a more efficient, stronger runner.

To maximise your ability to recruit your fast twitch fibres, you must incorporate strength training that works you to a high intensity (heavy loads). Without the right intensity, not all your fast twitch fibres are required to engage and therefore, you are limiting the benefits.

The reasoning behind this is that muscle fibres don't contract at varying percentages, instead they engage on an "all or nothing" basis.

When working with moderate weight, fewer fibres are engaging (although the ones that are, are engaging fully). Moving heavy weights (relative to your strength) requires recruiting as much muscle fibre as possible.

• How Do We Develop Strength?

To effectively build strength in a muscle or muscle group, it's fundamental to work them through a full range of motions. There are three points to consider when deciding how to perform a movement.

1. Maximise the weight that can be lifted i.e. maximise performance.

2. Maximise the work required by the muscles (positive stress).

3. Minimise the negative stress placed on the supporting structures.

Building strength is a balance between these three points and the importance of each depends on your goals.

If you perform a full-depth squat, it will maximise muscular effort, but it may also cause excessive stress on your knees and reduce the amount of weight you can lift.

On the other hand, a quarter-squat allows you to lift heavier loads with less stress on the supporting structures. However, your strength increase probably won't be as great, because the muscles aren't stressed through their full range of motion.

It all comes down to finding the optimal balance to achieve the best results for your body and chosen sport, and this varies from person to person, because their strengths and weaknesses differ.

In the following section, I have selected exercises that, together, produce highly effective strength programs for runners.

• Goblet Squat

Good athletes know that performance comes from the ground up. Your legs are your foundation and it is vital to build leg strength that will support everything you do.

The goblet squat is an awesome variation that will help you to develop your squat mechanics. As you sit back into a squat, your centre of mass shifts rearwards, so holding a weight to your front is a perfect counter balance.

The exercise was invented by strength coach Dan John and was named after way the weight is held: high at the chest, as if holding a large goblet.

When novices perform bodyweight squats with little depth and excessive forward tilt of their torso, coaches often try to rectify any perceived mobility issues the individual may have. However, stability, not mobility is often the underlying problem, as they compensate for their centre of mass shifting rearwards.

A coach should give the novice a weight to hold, and the goblet position makes a perfect counterbalance to the weight of the body moving backward. The weight removes many of the stability/balance issues they may be suffering and allows for greater depth to be achieved on the squat, as their torso remains more upright. Adding the goblet weight can literally progress someone with a terrible bodyweight squat to squatting well, within one set.

There is some debate regarding the correct depth for a squat. Some believe it necessary to go "ass to grass" and drop to a depth where the knees are fully bent. Others favour a depth where their hamstrings are just below parallel to the floor.

Joint anatomy and limb length can affect the way people squat. However, I consider it ideal to squat to the point where the hamstrings are just below parallel with the floor. In other words, the crease of your hips should dip just below the top of your knee caps. This maximises muscular engagement, while placing the minimum stress position on your knees and lumbar spine.

While a full-depth squat is essential for an Olympic lifter, the extra stress on the knees is not beneficial for runners.

For a goblet squat, a kettlebell is usually used, but dumbbells or plates also work well.

1. Squat down and grasp the handle of the kettlebell with both hands.

2. Lift the kettlebell and take a shoulder-width stance, with your toes pointing to the front or slightly outwards (no more than 30 degrees).

3. Initiate the movement with your hips, driving the glutes back.

4. As your hips hinge, bend your knees (almost simultaneously).

5. Lower under control, keep your knees in line with your toes.

6. Keep your elbows in, so that when you squat down, they comfortably fit in between your legs.

7. Once you have reached the appropriate depth (ideally, breaking parallel between your hamstrings and the floor), drive back up out of the squat.

8. Depending on the weight being used, complete 3-5 sets of 5-20 reps.

• Back Squat

There are many squat variations that are beneficial for runners, however the back squat will allow you to load the most weight and elicit the most strength gains.

During the back squat, the barbell is held on your upper back. There are two distinct placements, referred to as the *high bar* and *low bar* positions. Although each bar placement has its own effects on the mechanics of the back squat, we will work with the high bar variant, as it is a more accessible and comfortable position for most people.

High Bar Position: The barbell is held on the top of your traps, ensuring that it is *not* resting on the cervical vertebrae (distinct bony prominence on the back of the neck).

The barbell stays over your midfoot (halfway between your heel and toes, or the upper lacy part of the trainer) throughout the squat. If the barbell is high on your back, your torso requires less tilt to keep the barbell over the midfoot, so it stays more upright and allows for more depth.

During the high bar squat, leverage is weakest as you come up towards the parallel position (the point where your hips are most rearwards of the barbell). Making a conscious effort to drive your hips back under the barbell towards the end of the lift, brings you into a more mechanically efficient position. It maximises quad engagement and prevents your torso from falling forward.

Without enough quad engagement, individuals will often fall into the "good morning fault", where their glutes kick back, their knees straighten prematurely, and the load is lifted with the posterior chain alone. This places excess stress on the lower back and reduces the ability to lift heavier loads.

This is a complex exercise so make sure check out the free video at **http://geni.us/runners**

Always do one or two warm-up sets with an unloaded barbell to get accustomed to the exercise.

1. Set the barbell on the rack at upper chest height.

2. Grasp the barbell 1-2 palms wider than shoulder-width with a comfortable grip.

3. Move your head under the barbell, placing the barbell in position on your traps.

4. Walk under the barbell, so that your hips are directly underneath to ensure you don't lift the barbell off the rack with your lower back.

5. Lift the barbell up off the rack with your legs and take 2-3 short strides backwards – a long walkout wastes energy and increases the risk of injury.

6. Adopt your squatting stance. Experiment with various stance widths and see what feels best for you.

7. Take a big gulp of air, use the Valsalva manoeuvre, whilst bracing your core musculature.

8. As you brace your core, pull down on the barbell to help increase total body tension.

9. Initiate the squat with your hips, driving your glutes rearwards, and bend your knees.

10. Allow your knees to track directly over your toes (this will vary depending on limb length).

11. Sit back to the point where you break parallel and your hip crease dips just below the top of your knee caps, or as deep as you can go while maintaining good form.

12. Drive your feet into the floor and pull down hard on the barbell, as if you are trying to bend it over your back. This helps to maximise total body tension and muscular engagement.

13. Drive back up out of the squat.

14. Once you reach the top of the lift, exhale and get ready for the next rep.

15. When working with heavy loads, it's important that you treat every rep as a single, perfect movement.

16. Depending on the weight being used, complete 3-5 sets of 2-10 reps.

• Romanian Deadlift - RDL

One movement that is integral to human function and vital for the development of runners is the hip hinge.

The hinge plays a huge role during a squat. The hips hinge and the knees bend to facilitate the entire movement. Incorporating hinge exercises with varying degrees of knee bend maximises the work on the posterior chain – specifically the hamstrings and glutes. Therefore, the RDL is an essential exercise for runners.

The Romanian deadlift was developed by a Romanian weightlifter called Nicu Vlad. It is a fairly tricky exercise to describe in words, so once again, make sure that you watch the free video at **http://geni.us/runners**.

1. Start with the barbell at your hips (on a frame) with a pronated (over-hand) grip. Ensure you pick the barbell up with good form, while maintaining a neutral spine.

2. Initiate the movement by driving your glutes back and bending your knees slightly. Allow your shoulders to come over the barbell, while it maintains contact with your legs.

3. Keep driving your glutes back to facilitate the hinge and allow the barbell to track down your quads. If there is too much knee bend at this point, the barbell will sit on your quads, rather than track down smoothly.

4. Once the barbell passes your knee caps, bend your knees slightly to bring the barbell to about a palm's distance below your knees.

5. Engage the glutes and bring the barbell back up your legs, following the same path it went down. Maintain a vertical bar path throughout (if someone were watching from the side, they would see the barbell move in a vertical line).

6. Squeeze your glutes hard at the top to get them firing and proceed with successive reps.

7. Depending on the weight being used, complete 3-5 sets of 5-8 reps.

• Stiff Legged Deadlift

A true stiff legged deadlift (SLDL) begins with the barbell on the floor (hence "dead" lift, as it's a dead weight), and the barbell is lifted with stiff/straight legs. However, the variation I will be teaching in this section begins from the hips, similar to the Romanian deadlift.

This exercise will progressively strengthen your hamstrings through a full range of motion and will greatly reduce your risk of hamstring strain and increase your running performance.

1. The starting position for this lift is with the barbell at your hips with an over-hand grip, so ensure you pick the barbell up with good form, maintaining a neutral spine.

2. Hold the barbell at your hips with a soft knee position. Take a big gulp of air, use the Valsalva manoeuvre and brace your core musculature.

3. Slowly hinge and drive your glutes rearward, whilst allowing your shoulders to come over and slightly beyond the barbell. Really emphasise the hip hinge to maximise the engagement of your hamstrings.

4. As your hips hinge, ensure there is no change in your knee bend. Keep the barbell over your midfoot line.

5. As the barbell passes your knees, you will feel a lot of tension on your hamstrings. The range of motion you can achieve is dependent on the flexibility of your hamstrings.

6. When performed with a proper hinge, most people find that taking the barbell to a point between their knee caps and mid-shin is sufficient. However, some may require a greater range of motion. You can achieve this by standing on a raised platform.

7. Depending on the weight being used, complete 3-5 sets of 5-8 reps.

• Deadlift

The deadlift is the king of the hinge and pull movements, and is the key to the development of strong, powerful hips.

Please note that lifting a heavy weight off the floor can stress your spine in a way that can cause injury. It is essential that you perform this exercise with good form. Once again, refer to the free videos at **http://geni.us/ runners**.

It should be noted that injuries are not just a matter of technique or poor form. Regardless of whether you lift correctly or not, if your soft tissues haven't got the strength to handle the load (even with perfect form), injuries such as straining your lower back muscles can occur.

When it comes to the deadlift, many people are hell-bent on going as heavy as they can on every session, even if it's the first time they have lifted a barbell off the floor. However, to make real physical progression, you need to develop every link within the kinetic chain that is in your body and *progressive programming* will allow all your structures to adapt, remembering that some structures (particularly smaller muscles involved in joint stabilisation) may not develop as quickly as others.

The lower back is one of the most important links within the kinetic chain. Without strength in this area we not only compromise performance, but also risk serious, life-changing injury.

Do not underestimate the importance of the lower back – it truly is an integral part of your ability to maintain posture and maximise performance.

1. Set the barbell up on the floor with 45cm plates.

2. Approach the barbell so that your midfoot is directly underneath it. Your shins should be an inch away from the barbell.

3. Hinge with your hips and bend your knees until you can grasp the barbell.

4. Take an (over-hand) or alternated (one over-hand and one under-hand) grip.

5. Sit back with your glutes and drive your chest/ribcage up. This will bring your shins forward until they come into contact or are just off the barbell.

6. Take a big gulp of air, use the Valsalva manoeuvre, and brace your core musculature. As you do this, pull on the barbell slightly to create more tension.

7. Drive your heels into the floor and pull the barbell upwards and rearwards off the floor. Allow time for inertia of the bar to be broken. You must produce enough force to break the weight off the floor, and this doesn't always happen as soon as you start pulling.

8. Once the barbell passes your knees, drive your hips into it and push your chest up. Your shoulders will fall naturally behind the barbell. There is no need to shrug or throw your shoulders rearwards.

9. Once you have finished locking out your hips, drive your glutes rearwards and bend your knees slightly to allow the barbell to track down your legs smoothly (just like the RDL).

10. Once the barbell passes your knee caps, bend your knees until the plates touch the floor.

11. At the bottom, exhale and get ready for the next rep.

12. Don't bounce the plates off the floor to create upward momentum. Treat every lift as an individual rep.

13. Depending on the weight being used, complete 3-5 sets of 2-5 reps.

• Kettlebell Swing

The kettlebell swing is a *ballistic* hip hinge movement that develops explosive hip extension and will help to increase your running speed. Ballistic movements perform maximum acceleration and velocity over short periods of time. It is essential that both the upward and downward phases of this lift are completed with good speed.

Ballistic movements are commonly associated with injuries, because during a fast movement it is harder to maintain control and more stress is placed on the soft tissues. However, the actions we perform in sports like running, are generally ballistic in nature, so it's important to incorporate ballistic actions into your training.

There are two main styles of swings: the Russian swing, which brings the kettlebell to chest height, and the American swing, which brings the kettlebell overhead.

We will be looking at the Russian swing.

The true purpose of the kettlebell swing is to facilitate a ballistic extension of the hips. Once the kettlebell reaches chest height, you have achieved full extension and any further movement overhead simply detracts from this. If the kettlebell easily surpasses chest height, use a heavier weight to maximise muscle recruitment.

At the bottom of the lift (where the kettlebell is between your legs), your knees should be slightly bent. The kettlebell swing does not involve a squatting action

It works well to exhale at the bottom of the movement, while your ribcage and stomach are compressed, and inhale at the top of the movement, while your rib cage is expanded.

1. Place the kettlebell an arm's length in front of you.

2. Take a shoulder-width or slightly wider stance with soft knees. Hinge at the hips and drive your glutes rearwards. This will bring your torso just above parallel to the floor.

3. Grab the horn (handle) of the kettlebell.

4. Explosively pull the kettlebell rearwards into the back swing (kettlebell swung between your legs). Your arms should be high in your groin. If they are not, stress is placed on your lower back, rather than spread through your glutes and hamstrings.

5. Once the kettlebell has reached the end of the back swing, explosively contract your glutes and hamstrings to fire the kettlebell up to chest height.

6. From chest height, allow the kettlebell to swing back down in a fast, but controlled manner. Perform a full back swing (keeping your arms high in your groin) and continue with successive reps.

7. Depending on the weight being used, complete 3-5 sets of 5-20 reps.

• Alternate Rearward Lunge

All the exercises so far have been *bilateral*, meaning that both sides of the body are working in unison. The final three exercises in this chapter are *unilateral*, meaning they work each side (in this case the legs) independently.

Bilateral exercises allow you to load maximum weight and make the greatest strength progressions. Using both sides of the body together, you are generally more stable, and your neuro-musculature system can produce more force.

Single leg exercises are essential for runners, simply because running is a single-leg exercise.

You will notice that this and the following exercise are very similar, however there is a key difference between the two: during a lunge, both legs, regardless of their positioning, are involved in the movement. Usually the front leg holds around 75% of the weight, while the rear leg holds around 25%. During a split squat, one leg is used to complete the entire movement, while the other leg is almost 100% at rest, only giving a small degree of support.

Lunges can be performed forwards, backwards and laterally (out to the side), either moving in one direction (walking lunge) or in an alternating fashion, where you return to the same starting position each time.

I have chosen to use a backwards stride as it reduces the stress on your knees.

1. Place your feet a hip-width apart.

2. Take a reasonably long stride back with your right leg. Allow your right knee to drop comfortably towards the floor, while your left knee tracks forward slightly, while staying behind your toes.

3. It is fine for your right knee to gently touch the floor. However, try to avoid this to ensure tension throughout your body is not lost and that don't bruise your knee. I suggest keeping your knee 1-3cm off the floor.

4. As your front knee bends to facilitate the lunge, perform a slight hip hinge to ensure the movement maximises the engagement of your quads, hamstrings and glutes. This also ensures that your knee doesn't track too far forward.

5. Stride back to the original starting position.

6. Depending on the weight being used, complete 3-5 sets of 4-10 reps on each side.

• Front Foot Elevated Split Squat (FFESS)

Split squats involve setting up a pre-set stance and working the front leg in a squatting action.

Alternating the front leg and placing your weight on the front leg during the FFESS (just as with lunges) is a fantastic way to help mobilise the pelvis. The front foot elevation allows you to do this effectively without placing too much stress on the knees.

The front foot elevation is usually around 5-10 inches, but can be increased to knee height if used as a mobility drill to help ensure your pelvis is in a neutral position with good posture.

The FFESS not only effectively works the quads, glutes and hamstrings, but also acts to stretch the hip flexor of the rear leg, which can often be excessively tight. Tight hip flexors can cause lower back pain and result in reduced performance, due to their detrimental effect on hip extension.

This exercise can be performed with a barbell or dumbbells held at either side in a farmer's carry position.

1. Stand in a hip width stance, 2-3 foot lengths from a 5-10 inches platform.

2. Stride forward with one leg and place your whole foot flat on the platform, ensuring your knee doesn't track too far forward.

3. Lower yourself into a single leg squat, concentrating the load onto your front leg, while your rear leg provides support.

4. Lower to a depth that facilitates a stretch on the rear hip flexor, but not to a point where the stretch on the rear leg becomes detrimental to your ability to load the exercise.

5. Rise up and stride backwards to the starting stance. Complete successive reps using alternating legs.

6. Depending on the weight being used, complete 3-5 sets of 4-10 reps on each leg.

• Weighted Step Ups

Climbing stairs is essentially a more powerful version of walking and requires far more muscular engagement. When we increase the height of the step and add weight, it becomes a truly awesome exercise, not only for leg strength, but for overall conditioning too.

This exercise can be performed with a barbell, but also works well with a dumbbell held in either hand.

Step-ups can be worked on a moderate step of about mid-shin height. To increase the intensity of the exercise, increase the step to around knee height.

1. Stand a foot-length behind the box or step.

2. Stride upwards with your right leg, placing your entire foot onto the box.

3. Drive your right foot into the box and stride up with your left leg.

4. Once standing straight on the box, you can step back down, leading with your right leg.

5. A variation is to not place your left leg down, but drive your left knee up to hip height instead. This variation maximises hip extension on your right side and requires more stability.

6. Once back on the floor, this constitutes as 1 rep.

7. Lead with your right leg for half the reps, before completing the final half with your left leg.

8. Complete 3-5 sets of 4-10 reps on each side.

Chapter Five: Programming

• Introduction

This chapter takes the information from the previous sections and brings it together to create effective workout programs.

When programming, the easiest way to test an individual's strength is by a *one repetition maximum* lift or 1RM. This is the absolute maximum you can lift for one repetition. We then work off percentages of the 1RM to quantify the program. Testing a 1RM can be quite stressful on the athlete and comes with a certain risk of injury, especially if the athlete is not an experience lifter.

Due to this risk, coaches also work off an athlete's 2, 3, and 5RM, which are all much less stressful to test. To estimate your 1RM from your 2, 3, or 5RM, we use formulas or coefficients (although 1RM apps can be downloaded to your phone).

A coefficient is a constant number that is multiplied by the variable (weight lifted). These coefficients have been worked out over various studies and are surprisingly accurate.

The coefficient for a 5RM is 1.16 – so if your 5RM is 100kg, multiply that weight by 1.16 to find your 1RM. In this case, the 1RM would be 116kg.

Different coefficients and formulas give negligibly different results, but they all work well as estimations from which to program.

During basic development of strength, I have my athletes use the submaximal effort method, so they work at between 70% – 85% of their 1RM, and between 50% – 60% of their 1RM during dynamic effort movements (lifting with high acceleration and speed). This terminology is described in *Science and Practice of Strength Training* by Vladimir M. Zatsiorsky.

Another method to quantify your programming is the *rating of perceived exertion* (RPE) scale. This is simply a scale which rates your perceived level of physical effort. The simplest scale is a 1-10 rating with 1 being almost no exertion, 5 being moderate exertion, and 10 being the hardest it could possibly be for the number of reps programmed.

Both 1RM percentages and the RPE scale are used in the example 4-week program.

• Rest Periods

The main purpose of rest periods is to allow your breathing and heart rate to reduce. This allows substances that may impede training intensity to clear, whilst allowing substances that provide energy to restore.

Another important aspect of rest is to allow time for your nervous system to recover. This is especially important in strength training, specifically when working at maximal loads.

As a runner, you are probably used to taking as little rest as possible to try and improve overall fitness levels and recovery times. However, when strength training, you need to take sufficient rest periods to allow you to facilitate optimal work on each set, without taking so long that the fatigue from previous sets has completely worn off. In other words, successive sets should have a cumulative effect.

Recommended rest periods:

• When working above 85% of your 1RM, take 3-5 minutes rest between sets.

• When working between 70-85%, take 2-3 minutes rest between sets.

• When working below 70%, take 1-2 minutes rest between. However, anywhere up to 3 minutes on assistance work is fine, if needed. Remember that rest periods can be dynamic, depending on how you feel.

• Core work is best performed with short periods of between 10-30 seconds rest.

Let's begin with some pre-run activation, mobility, hip and core strength, and stability workouts. They are ideal sessions to add in pre- and post-run, or on rest days as active recovery.

• Pre-Run Activation

This routine acts as an ideal warmup to do before your run.

Exercise	Sets/Reps/Time	Rest	Notes
Banded Glute Bridges	2x20	20-30 Seconds	
Banded Lateral Walks	2x10 Strides – each side	20-30 Seconds	
Bodyweight/Goblet Squats	2x10	20-30 Seconds	
Alternate Rearwards Lunges/FFESS	2x6 – each side	20-30 Seconds	

• Mobility Regime

Foam roll the muscle for 30-60 seconds before selecting a stretch and perform that for 30-60 seconds.

Exercise	Sets/Reps/Time	Rest	Notes
Foam Rolling Calves & Stretches	2x30-60 Seconds - Each side	5-10 Seconds	Gastroc and soleus stretch
Foam Rolling Hamstrings & Stretches	2x30-60 Seconds – Each side	5-10 Seconds	
Foam Rolling Adductors & Stretches	2x30-60 Seconds – Each side	5-10 Seconds	
Foam Rolling Quad & Hip Flexors & Stretches	2x30-60 Seconds – Each side	5-10 Seconds	
Foam Rolling Glutes & Stretches	2x30-60 Seconds – Each side	5-10 Seconds	
Foam Rolling TFL	2x30-60 Seconds – Each side	5-10 Seconds	
Iron Cross Stretch	1x10 Reps – Each side		

• Hips and Core Strength and Stability

Complete this workout after a run or between runs.

Exercise	Sets/Reps/Time	Rest	Notes
Banded Glute Bridges	3x20 Reps	15-20 Seconds – 60 Seconds between exercises	
Birddog	1x10 Reps – Each side	20-30 Seconds	
McGill Curl Ups	3x5 Reps	20-30 Seconds	10 second pause at top
RKC Plank	3x30 Seconds	15-20 Seconds	
Side Planks	2x30 Seconds – Each Side	15-20 Seconds	

• Four-Week Training Program for Runners

Here is an example of a four-week cycle that consists of two training sessions a week.

The sessions are split between a primary squat day with hinge assistance exercises, and a primary hinge day with single leg assistance exercises.

I have programmed in some activation work prior to each session. However, activation or mobility work can be additionally programmed, where necessary, prior to sessions.

Don't waste too much time and energy on long warm-up sessions up prior to resistance training. Warming up with light sets of the primary movement or similar assistance exercise is usually sufficient. However, I do recommend working with the RAMP warmup protocol:

• **R**aise – heart rate and body temperature. This could be as simple as high knees or bodyweight squats. However, ideally you want the movements to be specific to the exercises you are going to be performing.

• **A**ctivate – key muscle groups you are using during the session (use any of the activation drills).

• **M**obilise – joints. You don't want to spend hours mobilising your whole body. Concentrate on areas that might limit your ability to perform a movement effectively. For example, mobilising areas that limit your ability to achieve a deep squat, or stretching your hip flexors prior to deadlifting allows you to facilitate stronger hip extension.

• **P**otentiate – Prime the body for maximal intensity i.e., progressively load the weight.

An example of ramping up for the back squat could be:

• 1-2 Sets with an unloaded barbell (5-10 Reps).

• 1 Set at 60% of the maximum weight you will be working at (5-10 Reps).

• 1 Set at 80% of the maximum weight you will be working at (3-5 Reps).

• Begin your 1st set of the programmed weight.

For this program, find out your 1RMs using the techniques in the introduction of this chapter. From there, work off the program percentages, but allow yourself 5% either side to allow leeway for good and bad days.

This program can be repeated. Simply increase the weight used progressively. After 8-12 weeks, retest your 1RMs and work off these new numbers. As you gain experience, add in new assistance exercises when necessary.

Finish the following program 1-2 weeks before any race, to allow time to taper. This does not necessarily mean ceasing all resistance training, but volume, intensity, and possibly frequency, should be tapered.

Week 1 – Session 1

Warm Up/Activation/Prehab:

Exercise	Sets/Reps (% / RPE)	Rest	Notes
Band Pull-Aparts & Front to Backs	3x10 of each exercise	Use front to backs as active recovery	
Terminal Knee Extensions	3x20 Each side	10 Seconds	
Goblet Squat	2x10 - RPE 6	20-30 Seconds	

Primary:

Exercise	Sets/Reps (% / RPE)	Rest	Notes
Back Squat	5x5 - 75%	2-3 Minutes	

Assistance:

Exercise	Sets/Reps (% / RPE)	Rest	Notes
RDL	4x8 - RPE 8	60-90 Seconds	

Core:

Exercise	Sets/Reps/Time	Rest	Notes
McGill Curl Ups	3x5	30 Seconds	10 Second pause at the top
RKC Plank	3x30 Seconds	15-20 Seconds	

Week 1 – Session 2

Warm Up/Activation/Prehab:

Exercise	Sets/Reps (% / RPE)	Rest	Notes
Band Face-pulls	3x10	20-30 Seconds	
Banded Glute Bridges	3x20	20-30 Seconds	
Banded Lateral Walks	3x10 Strides – Each side	20-30 Seconds	

Primary:

Exercise	Sets/Reps (% / RPE)	Rest	Notes
Deadlift	5x5 -75%	2-3 Minutes	

Assistance:

Exercise	Sets/Reps (% / RPE)	Rest	Notes
Alternate Rearward Lunges	4x6 – Each side - RPE 8	60-90 Seconds	

Core:

Exercise	Sets/Reps/Time	Rest	Notes
Birddog	3x5 – Each side	30 Seconds	
Side Planks	3x30 Seconds – Each side	15-20 Seconds	

Week 2 – Session 1

Warm Up/Activation/Prehab:

Exercise	Sets/Reps (% / RPE)	Rest	Notes
Band Pull-Aparts & Front to Backs	3x10 of each exercise	Use front to backs as active recovery	
Terminal Knee Extensions	3x20 – Each side	10 Seconds	
Banded Psoas March	3x10 – Each side	20-30 Seconds	

Primary:

Exercise	Sets/Reps (% / RPE)	Rest	Notes
Back Squat	5x5 -75-80%	2-3 Minutes	

Assistance:

Exercise	Sets/Reps (% / RPE)	Rest	Notes
SLDL	4x8 - RPE 8	60-90 Seconds	

Core:

Exercise	Sets/Reps/Time	Rest	Notes
McGill Curl Ups	3x5 -	30 Seconds	10 Second pause at the top
Pallof Iso Holds	3x40 Seconds – Each side	20-30 Seconds	

Week 2 – Session 2

Warm Up/Activation/Prehab:

Exercise	Sets/Reps (% / RPE)	Rest	Notes
Band Face-pulls	3x10	20-30 Seconds	
Banded Glute Bridges	3x20	20-30 Seconds	
Banded Stability Complex	3x5 of each movement on each side	20-30 Seconds	

Primary:

Exercise	Sets/Reps (% / RPE)	Rest	Notes
Deadlift	5x5 - 75-80%	2-3 Minutes	

Assistance:

Exercise	Sets/Reps (% / RPE)	Rest	Notes
FFESS	4x6 – Each side - RPE 8	60-90 Seconds	

Core:

Exercise	Sets/Reps/Time	Rest	Notes
RKC Plank	3x30 Seconds	15-20 Seconds	
Side Planks	3x30 Seconds – each side	15-20 Seconds	

Week 3 – Session 1

Warm Up/Activation/Prehab:

Exercise	Sets/Reps (% / RPE)	Rest	Notes
Band Pull-Aparts & Front to Backs	3x10 of each exercise	Use front to backs as active recovery	
Goblet Squat	2x10 - RPE 6	20-30 Seconds	

Primary:

Exercise	Sets/Reps (% / RPE)	Rest	Notes
Back Squat	5x3 @85%	2-3 Minutes	

Assistance:

Exercise	Sets/Reps (% / RPE)	Rest	Notes
RDL	4x8 - RPE 8	60-90 Seconds	
KB Swing	3x10 - RPE 7	60 Seconds	

Core:

Exercise	Sets/Reps/Time	Rest	Notes
McGill Curl Ups	3x5	30 Seconds	10 Second pause at the top
Birddog	3x5 – Each side	30 Seconds	

Week 3 – Session 2

Warm Up/Activation/Prehab:

Exercise	Sets/Reps (% / RPE)	Rest	Notes
Band Face-pulls	3x10	20-30 Seconds	
Banded Glute Bridges	3x20	20-30 Seconds	

Primary:

Exercise	Sets/Reps (% / RPE)	Rest	Notes
Deadlift	5x3 - 85%	2-3 Minutes	

Assistance:

Exercise	Sets/Reps (% / RPE)	Rest	Notes
Alternate Rearward Lunges	4x6 – Each side - RPE 8	60-90 Seconds	
Weighted Step Ups	3x6 – Each side - RPE 7	60 Seconds	

Core:

Exercise	Sets/Reps/Time	Rest	Notes
Pallof Iso Holds	3x40 Seconds – Each side	20-30 Seconds	
Side Planks	3x30 Seconds – Each side	15-20 Seconds	

Week 4 – Session 1

Warm Up/Activation/Prehab:

Exercise	Sets/Reps (% / RPE)	Rest	Notes
Band Pull-Aparts & Front to Backs	3x10 of each exercise	Use front to backs as active recovery	
Banded Stability Complex	3x5 of each movement on each side	20-30 Seconds	

Primary:

Exercise	Sets/Reps (% / RPE)	Rest	Notes
Back Squat	5x3 - 85%	3 Minutes	

Assistance:

Exercise	Sets/Reps (% / RPE)	Rest	Notes
SLDL	4x8 - RPE 8	60-90 Seconds	
KB Swing	3x10 - RPE 7	60 Seconds	

Core:

Exercise	Sets/Reps/Time	Rest	Notes
McGill Curl Ups	3x5	30 Seconds	10 Second pause at the top
Birddog	3x5 – Each side	30 Seconds	

Week 4 – Session 2

Warm Up/Activation/Prehab:

Exercise	Sets/Reps (% / RPE)	Rest	Notes
Band Face-pulls	3x10	20-30 Seconds	
Banded Glute Bridges	3x20	20-30 Seconds	

Primary:

Exercise	Sets/Reps (% / RPE)	Rest	Notes
Deadlift	5x3 -85%	3 Minutes	

Assistance:

Exercise	Sets/Reps (% / RPE)	Rest	Notes
FFESS	4x6 – Each side - RPE 8	60-90 Seconds	
Weighted Step Ups	3x6 – Each side - RPE 7	60 Seconds	

Core:

Exercise	Sets/Reps/Time	Rest	Notes
RKC Plank	3x30 Seconds	15-20 Seconds	
Side Planks	3x30 Seconds – each side	15-20 Seconds	

Conclusion

Life is busy and it can be a struggle to find time to train. Therefore, it is important that you maximise the efficiency of your training. The programme I have designed only requires two hours per week in the gym and will greatly improve your performance, whilst minimising your risk of injury.

Get into the routine of incorporating activation drills before your run, and mobility drills afterwards. Many of the activation, mobility and core exercises can be performed in your living room whilst watching TV, so it's simply a case of getting into the habit of doing them as they are not time consuming.

I hope this book compliments your running and benefits your overal physical fitness and physique. I hope it is helpful for you, and that it helps you to improve your ability and that you continue to love running.

Have fun!

Jay

Glossary of Terms

Anatomical Term	Definition/Description
Tendons	A flexible but inelastic cord of strong fibrous collagen tissue attaching a muscle to a bone.
Ligaments	A short band of tough, flexible fibrous connective tissue which connects two bones, and helps to hold a joint together.
Muscle Origin	The origin is the start of a muscle and is attached to the fixed bone, which is the one which doesn't move during the contraction.
Muscle Insertion	The insertion is where the muscle ends and is the point at which the muscle is attached to the bone moved by that muscle.
Pectoralis (Pecs) Major / Minor	Chest muscles – major (larger muscle) / minor (smaller muscle)
Deltoid (delts)	Shoulder muscles – anterior delts (front section) / medial delts (middle section) / posterior delts (rear section).
Rhomboids	Upper back muscles between the shoulder blades.
Trapezius (Traps)	Upper back muscle.
Latissimus Dorsi (Lats)	Mid- back muscle.
Diaphragm	A dome shaped muscle used in respiration.
Gluteals (Glutes) Maximus / Medius / Minor	The buttock muscles – major (largest muscle) / medius (middle muscle) / minor (smallest muscle). The gluteal muscles along with the TFL are also referred to as the hip abductors.
Piriformis	Small muscle underneath the gluteus maximus.
Hip Flexors Psoas Major / Iliacus	The muscles on the front of the hips.
Quadriceps (Quads) Rectus Femoris / Vastus Medialis / Vastus Intermedius / Vastus Lateralis	The four muscles of the thigh.
Peroneals Peroneus Longus / Peroneus Brevis	Muscles on the outer side of the lower legs.
Calves Gastrocnemius / Soleus	Muscles on the rear of the lower leg.
Achilles Tendon	Tendon on the back of the heel.
Plantar Fascia	Thick band of connective tissue on the sole of the foot.

Hamstrings Biceps Femoris / Semimembranosus / Semitendinosus	The three muscles on the rear side of the upper leg
Adductors	Muscles on the inner side of the thighs.
Tensor Fasciae Latae (TFL)	Muscle on the upper outer side of the thigh.
Iliotibial Band (ITB)	A band of connective tissue that runs down the outer side of the thigh.
Sciatic Nerve	A major nerve extending from the lower end of the spinal cord, through the glutes and down the back of the thigh.
Quadratus Lumborum (QL)	Muscles on wither side of the lower back.
Erector Spinae	Muscles that run up either side of the spine
Thoracic Spine	The thoracic spine is the twelve vertebrae between the base of your neck and the bottom of your rib cage. Often when we refer to the thoracic spine in a training environment, we are referring to the muscles which surround it.
Core Musculature	The musculature of your torso, but more specifically it is the lumbo-pelvic region (lumbar spine and pelvis, often referred to as your 'lower back'). These muscles are responsible for both stabilisation and the transfer of force from one of movement to the next, for example changing direction.
Transverse Abdominis (TVA)	The deepest muscle of the abdominal wall and is an integral component of the core
Abdominals Rectus Abdominis / Obliques	Muscles on the front of the abdomen – rectus abdominis (6 pack muscles) / obliques (muscles to the side of the rectus abdominis).

Technical Term	Definition/Description
Positive Stress	Physical stress that is adaptive and leads to improvements in physical performance.
Negative Stress	Physical Stress that is maladaptive and leads to injuries and regressions in physical performance.
Range of Motion (ROM)	The full movement potential of a joint.
Flexibility	This refers to a range of motion a muscle can achieve passively, essentially the length it can achieve.
Mobility	How freely a joint can move throughout its full range of motion actively. Flexibility is one very important aspect of mobility.
Release Techniques/ Myofascial Release	A method of hands-on therapy that you can perform yourself, usually with a foam roller or massage ball.
Muscle Tightness	This refers to the muscle-length. If a muscle is tight, then it is shortened. Some muscles have the tendency to be shorter and tighter, while others have the tendency to be longer and less activated.

Muscle Tension	Tension is often considered to be the same as tightness. However, not only tight or overworked muscles become tense. Muscles that are lengthened or weak can also become tense – examples of these will pop up throughout the book.
Activation	Getting a specific muscle working.
Strength	Strength is your ability to produce force, the more force you can produce to overcome a resistance (usually tested with a single effort), the stronger you are.
Muscular Imbalance	Occurs when opposing muscles provide different directions of tension due to tightness and/or weakness.
Compound Exercises/ Movements	Exercises which include multiple joints and muscle groups.
Single-Joint Exercises	Exercises which work a single joint to target a specific muscle.
Primary Lift	These are compound exercises. They are of most importance in terms of exercise selection as they work movements fully and require the most effort. Therefore, they should be trained first.
Assistance Lifts	Often referred to as *accessory exercises* are also compound movements. They are chosen to develop specific movements or muscle groups that help you to perform the primary lift or specific sporting actions.
Auxiliary Lifts	These single joint exercises. They are chosen to help develop your ability to perform the primary lift or specific sporting actions.
Concentric Phase/Contraction	The upwards phase of a movement, where the muscle(s) are shortening under tension.
Eccentric Phase/Contraction	The downwards phase of a movement, where the muscle(s) are lengthening under tension.
Isometric Contraction	A muscle contraction where there is no change in muscle length
Pronated Grip	Overhand Grip.
Supinated Grip	Underhand Grip.
Bilateral	Working both sides of the body at the same time.
Unilateral	Working one side of the body at a time.
Posture	A position which aligns your body so that minimal stress is placed on joints and the supporting muscles, tendons, and ligaments. This results in the stresses of daily life being distributed evenly.
Neutral Spine	A spine which is unbent and untwisted, with three natural curves.
Cervical Spine	Neck – should have a normal lordotic/inwards curve (lordosis).
Thoracic Spine	Mid-upper back – should have a normal kyphotic/outwards curve (kyphosis).
Lumbar Spine	Lower back – should have a normal lordotic/inwards curve (lordosis).
Sacrum & Coccyx	Back of the pelvis.
Neutral Pelvis	A pelvis which sits in the optimal position.
Lumbo-Pelvic Region	The lumbar spine and pelvis.
Low Back Pain	Pain, muscle tension, or stiffness localized below the costal margin (bottom rib) and above the inferior gluteal folds (bottom of your buttocks), with or without sciatica.

Anterior	Front of the body.
Posterior	Rear of the body.
Anterior Pelvic Tilt	Pelvis that tilts excessively forward.
Posterior Pelvic Tilt	Pelvis that tilts excessively rearwards.
Midline	Centre line of the body
Flexion	When the angle decreases between the two bones attached to either side of the joint being affected – bending a joint.
Lateral-Flexion	Side bending of the spine.
Extension	when the angle between the two bones increases – straightening a joint.
Anti-flexion/Lateral Flexion	Resisting forces that try to flex or laterally-flex your spine.
Anti-Extension	Resisting forces that try to extend your spine.
Anti-Rotation	Resisting forces that try to rotate your spine.
Protraction	Forward movements of structures of the body.
Retraction	Rearwards movements of structures of the body.
Adduction	Moving a limb laterally away from the midline.
Abduction	Moving limbs back in towards the midline from a lateral position.
Dorsi-Flexion	Refers to flexion at your ankle so that your toes are pointing upwards
Plantar-Flexion	Refers to extension at your ankle so that your toes point downwards towards the floor.
Pronation/Eversion of the Foot	This refers to when the weight it shifted to the inner side of the foot (soles facing outwards).
Over-Pronation	When your soles turn outwards slightly more than what is considered optimal, placing more load onto the inner side of the ball of your foot.
Supination/Eversion of the Foot	This refers to when the weight is shifted to the outer side of the foot (soles facing inwards).
Primary/Prime Mover	The muscle most responsible for completing an action.
Synergists	The muscle(s) which assist the prime mover.
Agonist	The muscle performing the action – the biceps during a biceps curl.
Antagonist	The muscles that produce an opposing joint torque to the agonist muscles – the triceps during a biceps curl.
Fixators & Neutralizers	These muscles help to stabilise the movement.
Secondary & Tertiary Movers.	Terms used to describe muscles which assist the prime mover (2nd and 3rd to). During compound lifts, often muscles that may not be considered the prime mover, might be producing just as much force to complete the action.
Diaphragmatic Breathing	Effectively using the diaphragm during respiration.
Nasal Breathing	Breathing through the nose.
Intra-abdominal Pressure (IAP)	Increased pressure in the abdomen caused by a held breath and contraction of the core muscles.

Valsalva Maneuver	A moderately forceful attempted exhalation against a closed airway. Like equalizing your ears on an airplane and blowing against a pinched nose.
Total Body Tension	Creating tension throughout the body by contracting muscles, using the valsalva maneuver and capitalizing on intra-abdominal pressure.
Anatomical Breathing	Synchronising your breathing with your movements
Biomechanical breathing	Breathing in before or during the eccentric phase, and breathing out during the later stages or after the concentric phase. This method increases total body tension.
Cadence	Stride frequency – the number of strides a runner takes in a minute.
Foot Strike	The way the foot lands while running.
Delayed Onset Muscle Soreness (DOMS)	The muscle soreness you feel days after a workout.
Golgi Tendon Organ	Receptor organ that senses changes in muscle tension. It can tell muscles to *shut off* when stimulated.
Proprioception	The body's ability to transmit a sense of position, analyze that information and react to it.
RAMP	A warmup protocol – refers to *Raise, Activate, Mobilise, Potentiate.*
Potentiate/Post-Activation Potentiation (PAP)	Potentiation in this context refers to the increase of strength in nerve pathways that have been used previously. Which in layman's terms, means that the associated muscles are primed and working at full capacity. We can use PAP to capitalise on an increase in neuromuscular efficiency – lighter loads often feel abnormally light after working with heavier loads.
Motor Unit	A neuron and the muscle fibres which it contracts.
Ballistic	Refers to movements that exhibit maximum acceleration and velocity over short periods of time. Essentially both the concentric (upwards) and eccentric (downwards) phases of this lift are completed with good speed.
Reps & Sets	*Reps* (repetitions) define the number of times you complete an exercise, and *sets* refers to how many times you will repeat that exercise for the specified number of reps. For example, 5 sets of 3 reps (5x3 – sets first), with 2 minutes rest between sets.
1 Rep Max (1RM)	Most you can lift for 1 rep. I usually work off *Training Maxes*, meaning there is no breakdown in form.
Maximal Effort Training	Maximal weight. Working above 90% of your 1RM
Submaximal Effort Training	Submaximal weight for submaximal reps. Working between 70-90% of 1RM – I usually programme between 75-85% of 1RM.
Repeated Effort Method	Submaximal weight for maximal reps – I usually programme between 60-75% for this method.

Dynamic Effort Method	Lifting at speed – Working between 50-60% of 1RM.
Training Frequency	How often you train.
Training Volume	How much you do in a session/workout.
Training Density	The work you can do in each amount of time. For example, 5x10 reps in 15 minutes is less density that 10x10 reps in 15 minutes.
Training Intensity	How hard you train. For example, how heavy you lift, or how fast you run.
Mind-Muscle Connection (MMC)	Consciously thinking about the muscle, you are working to increase its engagement.

Equipment	Definition/Description
Resistance Bands	Long resistance bands come in varying colours, which denote the tension of the band. Yellow: Low tension Red: Medium tension (recommended) Black: Medium tension (greater tension than red)
Small Loop Resistance Bands	Small bands are a great tool for hip and shoulder strengthening drills. The colours of these bands denote varying band tension. However, these colours can vary and therefore, I advise buying a set of 4-5 bands of varying tensions.
Foam Roller	A 90cm foam roller is ideal, (30-45cm rollers are also fine). However, if you choose to spend more you can purchase a 'rumble roller' which allows you to get deeper into specific areas.
Massage Ball	You can purchase balls designed specifically for massage, or use a lacrosse ball. Golf balls can be used (rolling the sole of the foot), but they're often too small to be truly effective. Peanut-shaped massage balls allow you to work both sides of your back, while avoiding pressure on your spine.
Barbell	The barbell is a 7ft long straight bar that weighs 20kg and can have weight plates attached to either side. Lower weight bars are available in some gyms (10-15kg).
Dumbbells	Dumbbells are a short bar with a weight (*bell*) at each end. Most gyms will have a wide selection of dumbbells in 1-2.5kg increments.
Kettlebell	A kettlebell is a large cast-iron ball-shaped weight with a single handle known as the *horn*. Kettlebells usually come in 4kg increments.
Plyo Box or Fitness Step	Strength & Conditioning gyms will usually have wooden plyo boxes which allow for three heights to be used (20/24/30 inch), and jerk boxes which stack various box heights. Most commercial gyms will have some form of plyo box, or fitness steps.

Equipment NB: All the equipment listed can be purchased on Amazon

Good Posture?

Do you struggle to maintain good posture?

My new book, *Fix Your Posture* contains over 70 effective, easy exercises that help reduce back pain and build the right habits into your daily life.

• A complete, simple exercise solution that corrects posture and alleviates pain.

• Extensive chapters devoted to fixing your neck, back, hips, legs and shoulders.

• Understand how each area of the body can become problematic and how to rectify each issue.

• 34 exercise tuition videos demonstrating how to optimally perform each posture-fixing exercise.

• Over 70 exercises with clear photos and instructions that will improve your posture and reduce pain.

Visit **www.fundamental-lifestyle.com** for further information

Printed in Great Britain
by Amazon